Unexpected Healers

Laurie M. Ingebritsen, M.S.

Fulton Books, Inc.
Meadville, PA

Published by Fulton Books 2020

ISBN 978-1-64952-405-8 (paperback)
ISBN 978-1-64952-406-5 (digital)

Printed in the United States of America

PREFACE

Horses have a way: a way of bringing us exactly what we need when we need it. They can make us laugh and cry within a single heartbeat. They can shed light on our flaws without making us feel the sting of judgment or shame. They have the power to influence our deepest beliefs and innermost emotions. And if we listen closely, a horse will always tell us where we need to grow, learn, or heal. They have the power to help us change our lives, heal our hearts, and strengthen our very being.

In my role as a master's level therapist, I was drawn to using horses in therapy for all those reasons. Using horses in therapy is called equine-assisted psychotherapy, and it was just starting to take hold in the 1990s. Slowly, clinicians were beginning to understand the positive impact that horses could have on the therapeutic process.

A few years after starting my private practice, I noticed a trend in women and children who had experienced abuse. They were having difficulty committing to behavioral changes that would progress them toward their goals, and they often found it challenging to change their perception of self or how they believed the world saw them. Some of these clients struggled to move forward at all; seeming to find safety in remaining in their old, unhealthy ways of being in the world.

I needed to find a way to help these clients break through to a new beginning. So, in 1999, my good friend and fellow clinician, Myra Darty, and I founded Equisense: an equine-assisted psychotherapy program for women and children. I brought my clients, she brought her horses, and we embarked on a journey neither of us would forget.

Almost overnight, I began to see significant differences between in-office and arena sessions. I watched as my clients flourished in the arena, and I was amazed at the behavioral changes they were willing to make with a horse at their side.

It seemed that every session had a certain "magic" about it. I began to see the horses do things that were out of character but always on point. They never failed to deliver exactly what was needed in just the right measure, and they seemed to be saying, "We've got this."

Under the horse's innate wisdom, I watched client after client get better faster and stay better longer. I watched women who were making no progress at all, completely change their lives after the lessons our horses imprinted on their hearts.

After years of watching the same scenarios unfold, I became convinced that the stories about our horses had the potential of not only helping the women and children who experienced them firsthand but those who will experience them vicariously by reading this book. (Note: To protect the identity of our clients, their real names and all identifying information have been removed.)

It initially made sense that the focus of this book would be about the women and children in our therapy program. But as each of their stories unfolded, I realized that horses don't just touch the lives of people in therapy, they have the potential to touch all the lives they interact with.

Therefore, this book needed to be about all women and all horses. It needed to be about how the horses' authentic, nonjudgmental way of being has the potential to heal, rejuvenate, and empower, and how the horse-human bond can open doors to self-understanding, personal growth, and forgiveness. Most of all, it needed to be about courage. The courage to trust another living being, the courage to face our demons, the courage to love, the courage to leave, and the courage to change—whether we are in therapy or not.

As I listened to women share their personal truths without holding back, I was humbled. They were willing to be vulnerable. They were willing to show their soft underbellies for the benefit of others. They were willing to trust that I would hold their experiences in my heart without judgment.

4

Therefore, the final chapters in this book are stories of my own. They are personal stories of how the horses in my life helped me learn to face my demons, love deeply, and live authentically. I included these stories as a way of thanking the women who so graciously shared their stories with me.

It is my hope that this book will touch the soul of every person who ventures within, and that they will vicariously receive the gifts they need most in their lives. It is with great joy that I invite you into these pages to experience the magic of the horse.

Part I
Women, Children, and Our Therapy Horses

To Jolly, Moonbeam, Lodur, Skjoni, and KB (the horses who gave their all); and to the women and children who taught us what it means to be courageous.

Thank you, Myra, for helping me start this amazing journey, and thank you, Betsy, for contributing your time, energy, and horses.

Finally, thank you to my amazing husband, David. Without your support, our beautiful facility never would have been built. Without you, this book could not have been written, and without you, my life would contain only a fraction of the humility, wonder, and gratitude that I hold deep within my heart.

CHAPTER I

Moonbeam's Shadow

Look back at our struggle for freedom,
Trace our present day's strength to its source;
And you'll find that man's pathway to glory
Is strewn with the bones of the horse.
—Author Unknown

O ne of the first women to enter our equine-assisted psychotherapy program was a perfect example of the horse's healing influence. We'll call her Cynthia. Cynthia had been seeing me in counseling for a couple of months, but her progress was minimal. By her own account, she had been in and out of therapy a few times and had been unable to affect any kind of sustainable change in her life. She was enmeshed in a chronically abusive relationship, and her fears and mental/emotional blocks were so severe that she was making little progress in traditional therapy. She had minimal awareness of self and was hyperfocused on pleasing everyone in her life.

Cynthia was thirty-two years old and one of those women who lived her life as a shadow-self—hiding from the light and unable to stand on her own. She was a woman who had been beaten down (literally and figuratively) by abuse: first, her parents, followed by an endless string of alcoholic ragers, and finally by her husband of eight years. The only position she knew to take was one of submissiveness, and even the idea of taking another stance created palpable anxiety for her. And that was understandable, given her history. Standing up for herself had always been a dangerous option. Passivity and flying under the radar had become her only tools for survival.

Cynthia lacked the insight to see how her own attitudes and behaviors were getting in the way of her healing, which is another common factor for women with abuse histories. Because of this, we chose one of my colleague's horses, Moonbeam, as our equine partner. Moonbeam liked to push people around. She was one thousand pounds of in-your-face attitude and a me-first disposition. She had little regard for rules, and in short, she was very much like almost everyone else in Cynthia's life.

To the untrained eye, pairing a passive female with a pushy horse might seem like offering a lamb up for slaughter. But to the experienced eye, it was offering Cynthia one of the only safe ways out. Cynthia lived in a reality in which standing up for herself, without the proper support, could put her life in danger. Many women are killed every year in their attempts to leave an abusive situation or to stand up to the abuser on their own.

For Cynthia, the goal of equine therapy would not be to encourage her to overtly stand up to her abuser. Rather, we hoped that she would gain newfound strengths that would enable her to envision a better, safer life, to create healthy boundaries and assertive abilities that would empower her to seek help within the community and actively take the steps necessary to safely remove herself from abusive situations.

It was our hope that the "re-creation" of relationship dynamics that Moonbeam would offer Cynthia would be a healing catalyst in her journey. Through successful interactions with Moonbeam in a safe and supportive environment, Cynthia would have an opportunity to adopt a healthier perspective: a perspective created from witnessing her own behaviors in action. Ultimately, we hoped that she would witness her own power to effect change and that she would begin to believe that she deserved something better.

That was a lot of hoping on our part because Cynthia had been abused for so long that she had begun to shut down. Her sense of personal boundaries, and even her awareness that she was being abused, had begun to erode. Therefore, our initial approach with her was to increase her awareness related to how her passivity was keeping her a victim. Understanding that she played a role in remaining in an abusive cycle was a critical step in empowering her to create change.

Our initial arena session with Cynthia is permanently etched in my memory. First, because it was the hottest day of the year—triple digits without an inch of shade—and second, because what happened in the arena that day made me forget the heat. Cynthia had been reluctant to enter the arena because of a long-standing fear of horses, and an even longer standing distrust of humans. You don't have to be pathologically passive for a thousand pounds of intimidating horseflesh to give you pause, but Cynthia's chronic fear of anything more powerful than herself certainly played a role in her reticence. And her understandable distrust of humankind gave her no sense that our presence would offer a safe haven. In her own time, and to her credit, she entered the arena. This was no small feat when you imagine that she might have felt as if she was walking into the jaws of death with no one to save her.

As Cynthia entered the arena, I offered her Moonbeam's lead rope, which she limply accepted, and we began our hour as if it were any other session.

Moonbeam lost no time in asserting her presence. Her nose immediately entered Cynthia's personal space and she began sniffing, prodding, and pushing. Cynthia didn't acknowledge the horse's behavior, and never made eye contact with her. I watched the interaction, or maybe I should say lack of interaction. I was fascinated by Cynthia's total lack of response to her equine charge. Finally, Moonbeam gave her a big push but still not as much as a flinch from Cynthia.

I stopped action, which is a time-out technique we used to help a client notice or process an interaction they are having with the horses.

"Cynthia, do you mind if we stop for a moment?" I asked. "I'm noticing that Moonbeam has been putting her nose in your space and pushing on your chest for quite a while now. How do you feel about that?"

Cynthia shifted her gaze from me to the horse, as if seeing her for the first time. With the lead rope still held limply in her hand,

and the horse still pushing on her chest, she said, "Oh, she was? I didn't notice."

My internal dialogue went something like this, *Didn't notice? One more push and she'd have knocked you off your feet. Your shirt is full of horse spit and I'm fairly sure she's cleaned out your pockets!* I was, quite frankly, astonished. All the in-office therapy sessions hadn't even begun to shine light on the depth of Cynthia's ability to tune out and shut down. I said out loud, "I wonder what's causing you to block that out?"

An automatic nervous giggle emerged from her throat. "I don't know," she said. "She's not really bothering me." Excusing the abuser and putting the abuser's needs before their own are common characteristics of women who have experienced chronic abuse.

"Hmm," I said. "I think it might bother most people if someone came into their space uninvited and pushed them around." And then I offered her the first chance to make an active choice. "Now that you've noticed that she's in your space uninvited, what would you like to do about it?"

"What do you want me to do?" she asked. Fear of making a choice and being responsible for that choice is also common among women who have learned to be afraid of other people's disappointment or anger. They believe that their safety depends on pleasing, acquiescing, and deferring.

"It's not about what I want. The choice is yours. Are you happy with her being in your space uninvited?"

"No," she said, as she began to lightly stroke Moonbeam's face (who, by the way was still being pushy). In effect, by petting Moonbeam while she was pushing on her, Cynthia was reinforcing the negative behavior. I chose to help her see how her response to Moonbeam was contributing to the problem.

"So, you don't want her in your space, but you are rewarding her for being there."

"Oh, ha...I didn't think of it that way," she said, withdrawing her hand.

"You don't want her there, and you've decided not to reward her. Is there anything else you'd like to do about it?"

"No."

"What will happen if you do nothing?"

"She'll keep pushing on me."

"Besides doing nothing, I wonder what other choices you might have."

"I could ask her to move."

"What do you think might happen if you did that?"

"She would get mad."

"And then what would happen?"

"She would hurt me."

Cynthia's eyes welled up with tears, and I could see that she was beginning to make a connection between her moment with this horse and her real-life abuse story. It was time to help her take the next step. "You don't want Moonbeam to take advantage of you, but you are afraid that if you ask for what you need, or you don't let her have her way, she will get mad and become even more pushy. Is that right?"

"Yes," she said as her gaze traveled to her shoes.

"It can be scary to think that standing up for what you need might put you in danger," I said. "It might feel easier to ignore her or try to please her. What's happening here with Moonbeam…is it similar or different than things that have happened in your real life?"

Asking clients to make a solid connection between the undeniable truth they are enacting in the arena and their real lives is a powerful request, and it's one that often brings them to a crossroads. If they cannot deny the truth of what's happening in the arena, then they must also face the existence of that truth in their real lives.

All the years of trying to stay safe and trying to avoid the inevitable aggression of those she should be able to trust culminated in the next few moments. Cynthia's spine gave way to the pressure she'd been carrying her entire life. As she slumped to the ground, massive sobs began to emanate from her small frame. She sat on the ground, still holding limply to the lead rope, and recounted her story of endless beatings and her fear-filled existence.

Cynthia's ability to tell her story was a monumental step forward. It was a gateway to the cleansing of spirit and the first step toward the possibility of a new beginning. The sadness, fear, anger, and guilt that made their way to the surface, were signs that she could now begin the healing process.

After some time, Cynthia stood up.

"What do you want to do?" I asked.

"I want her out of my space," she said. "I want HIM out of my space," referring to her current husband.

"Can you tell her that?" I asked. Cynthia wiggled the lead rope (a technique we taught her for getting the horse to back up). "Get out of my space," she said in an almost-inaudible whisper. Moonbeam didn't budge.

"I don't think she heard you. You have spent a long time letting her have her way today. You might need to make a point here."

Cynthia wiggled the rope harder. "Get out of my space," she said. This time we could hear the determination. That got Moonbeam's attention, but Moonbeam, being Moonbeam, stood her ground.

"This is your space, and she has no right to be in it uninvited," I said. I encouraged her to get as big as she needed to get in order to be heard.

And suddenly, this wisp of a woman mustered up everything she had. "GET OUT OF MY SPACE!" she screamed, this time flailing her arms and stomping her feet. And crying. Moonbeam stepped back.

"I MEAN IT! GET OUT!" Moonbeam took another step back, as if on cue.

Cynthia had just done something that she'd never done in her life. She had claimed her space and her right to it. I wanted to help her process this important moment, so I offered a brief summary. "Allowing others into your space, or keeping them out, is a choice that you have the power and the responsibility to make. How would it sound to you if, from now on, Moonbeam came into your space only when you invited her?"

"Good," she said and gave a long cleansing sigh. So did Moonbeam. Cynthia invited Moonbeam in for a pet. "Goodbye, Moonbeam," she said. And under her breath, she whispered, "Thank you."

Giving voice to reality doesn't make the pain of that reality magically disappear, nor does it automatically create the ability to be assertive or to safely get out of a dangerous relationship. But it does help to create a backdrop of truth from which to proceed. Cynthia's life experiences had created insecurity, fear, and self-questioning. Her equine journey took five sessions, and at the close of our fifth session, she had identified reasonable boundaries and was able to clearly ask for what she wanted. She had developed a safety plan and was ready to make the next step.

Cynthia still had a long road ahead of her, but she had gained insights that allowed her to realize her right to safety. With the help of a local victims' support group, she and her son were able to leave the abusive relationship and move to safe housing.

As is common for clients who work with horses, Cynthia kept in touch for quite some time. At last report, she had not returned to the abusive relationship and was continuing to make strides in planning a life for herself and her son.

Thank you, Cynthia, for allowing us to witness your courage, your strength of character, and your perseverance. Thank you, Moonbeam, for knowing exactly what she needed and in what measure. What years of counseling could not penetrate, you penetrated in a single moment in time.

CHAPTER II

Lodur, The Secret Keeper

"I don't like people," said Velvet.
"I only like horses."
—Enid Bagnold, *National Velvet*

My equine-assisted therapy program eventually began to expand and about seven years after its inception, I had branched out on my own and built a small equine center on some property near my home. I had expanded the equine program to include couples, families, sports teams, and children. That was when I met Simone, a seven-year-old girl who had been placed in residential treatment after her caretakers were charged with abuse. Prior to coming to the center, she had refused to speak a word about the horrendous treatment she suffered in their care.

Simone was becoming more withdrawn and had frequent periods of melancholy. Understandably, she had a well-developed mistrust of adults and abjectly refused to talk about her feelings with them. She had recently begun having violent outbursts and was physically assaulting other children.

It's not uncommon for abused children to recoil when given the opportunity to tell their stories. Many of them carry secrets of abuse well into adulthood, fearing that disclosure will result in harm to themselves or someone they love. They often believe that the abuse was their fault, and that talking about the atrocities will only serve to shed light on their shame. They bottle up their pain until it silently and systematically eats away at the core of their being.

The first day that Simone arrived at our facility, she was accompanied by Kendra, a staff member from the children's home. I was immediately struck by the old soul I saw staring at me through oversize glasses. Her small frame seemed to be taken over by the goggle-like spectacles. I couldn't help but chuckle (on the inside) at her comical presentation.

"Hello, Simone. It's nice to meet you," I said, as I squatted down to meet her at eye level.

"Hullo," she said, quietly.

"Do you like horses?" I asked, knowing what the answer would be.

"Uh huh. Do you have one?" she asked.

"I do. His name is Lodur. Would you like to meet him?"

"Uh huh," she said, and her face lit up…ever so slightly. Simone, Kendra, and I stepped into the arena, where Lodur was waiting.

At first observation, Lodur seemed like any other horse. But to those who knew him well, he was truly one-of-a-kind. He was a fifteen-year-old Icelandic that had the most soulful eyes I'd ever seen. More than once, I'd watched him use his quiet nature and gentle spirit to touch the heart of an aching person, and I was hoping that this time would be no different.

The instant that Simone spotted him, her demeanor changed. This slightly melancholy, waiflike child transformed into a smiling ball of light. She took off across the arena without asking, and I held my breath. As wonderful as Lodur was, he had one flaw: he sometimes succumbed to a case of stranger danger. This would not be a good time for him to choose to be antisocial.

Luckily, my fears were unwarranted. "Can I pet him?" she asked, as her hand was contacting his plentiful black mane.

"It looks like Lodur thinks that's a good idea," I said.

"I wish I could live here," she said spontaneously, as she proceeded to tenderly touch his face and neck.

As she busied herself with the task of horse-human bonding, she turned to Kendra and said, "Can I live here, instead of at the center?" Hello, Lodur; goodbye children's home!

Simone had been diagnosed with an attachment disorder and attachment disordered children often lack boundaries. They tend to attach too quickly and too intimately with others. The flip side is that they can just as quickly detach from them. Simone's leap into a devotion to Lodur, and her simultaneous willingness to sever all ties with the children's home, demonstrated both tendencies in one fell swoop.

Kendra's reply was a careful one. "Um, well, you are going to get to come here and visit with Lodur a few times. Would you like that?"

"Yep...but I'd rather live here," she said, as she stroked his face and looked into his eyes.

Horses live in the present, and they have the uncanny ability to take each event at face value. For children like Simone, who are so often confronted with rejection and loss, this was truly a gift.

Because Lodur didn't have the ability to judge Simone's behavior as right or wrong, he could respond to her without prejudice. He graciously allowed her touch and returned the gesture by gently wiggling his lips across the top of her hand.

I don't know exactly what Simone felt in that moment, but I'm guessing that at least part of her felt authentic acceptance from another being. Whether driven by a pervasive attachment disorder, or simply a natural bond between child and horse, it was obvious that the two had made a connection. And for the time being, that's all that mattered.

After a time, I (somewhat reluctantly) broke into this silent love affair. "Do you know why children come to see Lodur?" I asked.

The spectacles turned toward me. "To brush the horses?"

"Yes, to brush the horses. And sometimes, while we're brushing horses, we talk about things that are on our minds."

"I don't have anything on my mind," she said with a certain matter-of-factness that implied I probably shouldn't go there.

"Oh," I said. "Okay. Then we'll just brush."

"Okay, then."

"Okay."

So brush we did and talk we didn't. And that was the end of our first day.

CHAPTER III

Pick a Card, Any Card

Let a horse whisper in your ear and breathe
on your heart. You will never forget it.
—Author Unknown

Simone's second visit started out on a different note than the first. She came in the door animated and eager to get to the arena.

"Are we going to pet Lodur today?" she asked.

"Yes, and we're going to ask him to help us talk about some things today." I could see that the mere mention of a "discussion" was somewhat threatening.

"Oh," she said. She moved past me without another word, and silently grabbed the grooming bucket. She wasted no time in collecting Lodur and starting the grooming task. I matched her strokes with a brush of my own and we checked in for the day.

"How has your week gone?" I asked.

"Fine, but I don't really want to talk about it."

During a phone call prior to Simone's appointment, Kendra had filled me in on the fact that she had become increasingly aggressive with others during the week. It was no surprise that she didn't want to open that bag of worms.

"Okay, you don't have to talk about it, if you don't want to," I said. "Do you mind if I talk to you though?"

"That's okay," she said, although I had the distinct impression that she intended to put strict boundaries on the subject matter.

"Okay, thanks," I said. "Kendra mentioned that you've been having some trouble keeping your hands to yourself this week. Sometimes, when people don't feel good, their feelings come out of their arms and legs."

"What?" She momentarily forgot her vow of silence. "Feelings can't come out of our arms and legs!" She was laughing at the thought.

"Sure, they can. Every time we hit or kick or push someone, our feelings are coming out of our arms and legs. We do need to get our feelings out of us, or they can make us feel sick. But when they come out of our arms and legs by hitting or kicking, then we cause other people to feel bad."

Simone silently kept brushing.

Silence is often a nonverbal way of disengaging; but being the fearless therapist that I liked to think I was, I ventured even deeper into the verbal void.

Almost as if talking to myself, I said, "I wonder if there is a place on our body that would be better at helping us tell people how we feel?"

She broke her silence once again. "I don't know." She was brushing the same spot over and over, so I could tell that I had hit a nerve.

"What do you think would happen if a person chose to let their feelings out through their mouth instead?" I asked.

"Well…they would probably get in trouble."

"What would happen?" I asked.

"Well…I don't know. Get hit maybe. Or maybe yelled at."

"That wouldn't make someone feel very safe, would it?"

"Nope." She was still brushing, only now she moved to Lodur's face. She seemed mesmerized as she repeatedly slid the soft brush between his eyes.

I let them have this moment, and then reconnected.

"Kendra tells me that you don't like talking about your feelings at the center. Do you think it's possible that your feelings are starting to come out of your arms and legs?"

"Maybe, but that's okay," she said. Simone was beginning to push against my therapeutic prodding. Abused children will often retreat if they feel threatened, and I sensed that Simone was starting her move toward safety. I needed to join her in this quest.

"It probably feels safer to have our feelings come out of our arms and legs," I said.

"Yeah."

"Talking to grown-ups about how you feel just might not feel safe."

"Yeah." Her hand held the brush as it continued to float up and down the same spot on Lodur's face. Some horses may have objected to her diligence, but Lodur stood stock still. If he wished he were somewhere else, he never let on.

"What if you could talk to Lodur instead?" I asked.

"Lodur? Can he talk?" She stared back at me in surprise, her too-big glasses falling off the bridge of her nose.

"Lodur doesn't talk like people do, but he's a great listener. And one of the reasons I like him is that he won't tell anyone what you say to him. He's great at respecting your privacy."

Simone seemed open to this idea of talking to a nonhuman. "Are you going to talk to him too?" she asked. I was fairly sure that this question meant I was not invited.

"Nope. It's just between you and Lodur."

"Okay, and I'll take him way over there." She pointed to the far corner of the arena.

"Okay," I said. "That sounds like a nice private place to talk. Do you know what you want to talk to him about?" I asked.

"Nope."

"Well, let's see…we know that your arms and legs have been pretty busy telling people how you feel lately. Maybe you could practice using your mouth and talk to Lodur about your feelings."

In the moment of complete silence that followed, I was concerned that I may have caused her to shut down. Children who hold their feelings close to their chest can be sensitive to overt attempts to help them talk. Working with horses usually gave us a little more latitude, but you just never knew when something that worked before might backfire.

Finally, she responded. "Yeah, I could do that. He would like that."

I breathed an internal sigh of relief. "I have some Post-It notes here. What if you wrote down the feelings you want to talk with him about? Then, if you don't finish today, they'll help you remember where you left off. You could put one feeling on each piece of paper. Would that work?"

Her willingness to proceed surprised me a little, but we were obviously on a roll. Understandably, she still needed reassurance that all of this was only to occur between herself and Lodur. "I'm going to take my papers and pencil to the corner. C'mon Lodur," she said, and horse and child moved in unison to the farthest corner of the arena.

Kendra and I waited as Simone diligently wrote her feeling words on the Post-It notes. When she was finished, she returned with seven pieces of paper.

"We probably only have time for you to talk with him about one or two of your feelings today," I explained. "Can you pick the one you want to start with?"

"I can't decide. I think I'll let Lodur choose," she said as she shoved all seven pieces of paper out in front of her, her arms fully extended. She reminded me of a magician asking his subjects to "pick a card, any card." Lodur stood looking at her from about ten feet away.

My heart was in my throat. Horses are wonderful therapeutic partners, and most of the time everything works out as it should. However, there are those rare occasions when best laid plans fall short. Horses are horses, after all: wonderful, insightful, honest, and unpredictable. It was the unpredictable part that was worrying me at that moment.

Simone had put all her faith and trust into this animal, and I knew that he wasn't about to help her make a choice. How could he? We were at a critical juncture. If Lodur failed to comply, the bond that had been quickly made could be just as quickly broken. He could become yet another being that had let her down. She might disconnect from him like a plug from a socket. Game over.

My therapist's brain was reeling as I tried to think of a quick recovery, but what happened next sent me reeling in a whole new way. A shiver ran up my spine as I watched Lodur begin to approach Simone. I held my breath as he moved in like a man on a mission, and without hesitation, placed his muzzle on one of the seven pieces of paper. He didn't grab it, lick it, or eat it. He simply touched it with the soft end of his nose and stood there as if to say, "How's that?" "Okay! That's the one then," Simone said. Her response was that of a person who held absolute faith in her partner. All at once, I felt disbelief and awe. I was humbled and extremely grateful.

Simone moved off across the arena with Lodur in tow and the rest of her papers stuffed in her pocket. She took her time, talking quietly to him with her head against his neck. As they walked back toward me, I saw her reach into her pocket and her hand emerged with the crumpled pieces of Post-Its.

"How was that?" I asked.

"Good. He's a good listener. He likes me to tell him about my feelings. I'll do another one." One thing I was beginning to learn about Simone was that she didn't have a problem asserting herself.

Time was running short, but she was the last client for the day, so I kept my timekeeper comments to myself. I watched her hold out the remaining six feelings, waiting for Lodur to help her just as before. And right on cue, he picked another card from the mix.

When Lodur and Simone met the following week, the scenario repeated itself five more times. Lodur picked every feeling for Simone in succession, and each time, the two retreated to their private corner.

Simone had a total of four sessions with Lodur, after which she was able to talk about her feelings with the staff at the children's home. The last time I checked in with them, her aggressive behaviors were lessening, and she was making steady progress.

Thank you, Lodur, for being Simone's partner in finding her voice and for keeping her secrets while she learned to be safe.

CHAPTER IV

Truth Lies Where Fear Subsides

The horse will teach you if you will listen.
—Ray Hunt

I can't say that we were always experts at knowing why a horse would make a good match for a client; sometimes it was just intuition. But in this case, we chose KB to be our equine partner because we believed she would help build our client's confidence. Little did we know that it would be so much more than that.

KB was a sixteen-hand retired show horse, who was beautiful in spirit but just a tad worn down by life. No longer in her prime, she spent her days flying under the radar; presumably so that she could pursue her favorite pastime—standing still. It was not uncommon to find her sleeping on the job, and her gentle demeanor put clients at ease. We decided that she would be an excellent choice for our timid client. And during the first session, she didn't disappoint.

Jennifer was thirty-four years old and a little like KB. She was a tall, pretty woman, with a gentle way about her. And like KB, she spent a lot of her time trying not to attract attention and was a little worn around the edges.

Like so many of our female clients, Jennifer had suffered years of verbal and physical abuse and had entered counseling because her eight-year-old son and five-year-old daughter were being verbally abused and physically threatened. She was becoming increasingly worried that, if she didn't do something, things were going to escalate. She was afraid that she would no longer be able to keep herself and her children safe.

On her first visit, Jennifer openly expressed her fear of horses, and her anxiety about working with KB was evident. A sixteen-hand horse stands quite tall, so choosing to interact with KB took some courage on Jennifer's part.

Jennifer's first task involved getting to know her equine partner. This can help a timid person gain confidence and begin to bond with the horse. As part of the getting-to-know you process, we asked Jennifer to groom KB and pick out her feet. The grooming portion can help to calm an anxious person and picking up a horse's foot helps to build trust and leadership skills.

Jennifer tentatively began the task of grooming, making gentle sweeping motions with a soft brush along KB's back. As she brushed, she seemed to be nonverbally "checking-in" with KB by looking over her shoulder to see what KB's other half was doing. The closer she got to KB's hindquarters, the more frequent the check-ins became. Something about this behavior suggested that it might have more to do with life outside the arena than with the task at hand.

"How's that going for you?" I asked.

"Okay," she said, but her response was littered with anxiety. I decided to let the situation play out a bit more. Jennifer took several more minutes to finish the task of grooming to her satisfaction.

"How was that?" I asked

"It was okay. She sure is big…much taller than me!"

"She is. How do you feel about interacting with a horse who is so much bigger than you?"

"It's kind of scary, but kind of cool at the same time. At least I did it!"

"You did. That probably took some courage. The final stage of the getting-to-know you game is to pick out her feet. Is that something that you are willing to try?"

"Umm…do I have to?" She had stopped blinking. (It's interesting that both horses and humans stop blinking when faced with stressful situations.) "Nope."

Underneath Jennifer's fearful appearance was a strong woman, which is really no surprise. After all, it must take more than a bit of courage to go home every night to a situation that holds a constant threat to your personal safety.

"Well, I don't think you'd ask me to do it if I would get hurt, so okay, I guess," she said. (It's important to note that Jennifer and I already had a therapeutic relationship prior to her first day in the arena, so her willingness to trust me was based on our experience together so far.)Many people have trepidations about picking up a horse's hoof, so Jennifer's willingness to persevere led me to believe that she was not a person who gave up easily. However, as she worked on KB's feet, I noticed that her over-the-shoulder check-ins were increasing. When you hold a horse's hoof, your back faces the horse's head and you are slightly bent over at the waist. That means that you have control over the foot, but the biting end of the horse is at liberty to do as it pleases, or at least that is how a novice might see it.

As Jennifer attempted to pick out KB's hoof (which KB had willingly given her), she repeatedly looked back at KB's head. As time went on, I could see that tears were beginning to well up in her eyes. The more she checked, the more she seemed to need to check. It didn't take long before her tears transitioned into quiet sobs. Now it was time to help her process what was happening.

"Jennifer, I'm noticing that you are looking back over your shoulder quite a bit. Can you tell me what's going on for you?"

"I'm afraid that she's going to hurt me."

"Has she given you any indication that she's going to hurt you?" I asked.

"No, but that doesn't mean she won't."

"It's a possibility," I said. "But horses usually give us a warning before they let us have it."

She paused a moment, seeming to take in the rationality of my response.

"I'm just afraid that if I take my eyes off of her, she'll bite me."

"You don't trust that you are safe, and you feel as if you have to keep up a constant vigil."

"Yes."

"Do you keep up a constant vigil in your real life as well?"

At this point, Jennifer stood up and began methodically rubbing KB's back. "I just never know when he is going to go off." She had seamlessly transitioned from talking about KB to talking about her husband.

"It seems like the second I let my guard down, he strikes. I never know when he is going to rage or hit me for no reason at all. One minute everything will be fine, and the next minute he's beating me black and blue. Or he's going after the kids."

"So, in your real life, when people give you signals that everything's okay, you've learned not to trust them."

"Yeah…I guess so."

"I have some good news for you. That's not how it works with horses. What you see is what you get. They're always honest, and they have no hidden agendas. If KB is telling you that she's content, it's okay for you to believe her."

Jennifer's shoulders relaxed a little, but it was evident that she only partially believed me. "How do I know if she's content?"

"That's a good question, and it makes sense that you would want to know that. You've spent a lifetime needing to know the signs of impending danger, and it has become a survival strategy for you. In times when you are truly in a threatening, volatile situation, you need those skills. But you don't need them here. It might take a while for you to know that, and that's okay."

We gave Jennifer some pointers for reading equine behavior and ended for the day.

My partner and I thought that this was a pivotal session for Jennifer, but we had no idea that the following week would prove to be the real turning point. We also had no idea that it would be KB who led the session, or that we would simply be observers of KB's newly found kick-butt strategies.

CHAPTER V

I Will Follow You

Master said God had given men reason by which they could find out things for themselves, but he had given animals knowledge which did not depend on reason and which was much more prompt and perfect in its way, and by which they had often saved the lives of men.

—Anna Sewell

Jennifer arrived for her second session eager to begin her interactions with KB. The week between sessions had given her time to reflect on the insights that KB had helped her illuminate. Jennifer admitted that, although she was still nervous, anticipation and motivation were starting to bubble to the surface. In one short session, her eyes had been opened to the possibility that she could see her life unfolding in a new way.

"No looking over my shoulder today," she said as we made our way into the arena.

"Deal," I said, returning her smile and handing her KB's lead rope.

Because of Jennifer's level of anxiety the previous week, we opted to give her a few moments to reconnect with KB. It was obvious that she was beginning to bond with this gentle giant. We spent a few moments asking Jennifer to review the body language she was noticing, and she concluded that KB was relaxed, tuned-in, and in a cooperative mood.

"Time for feet?" I asked.

"Time for feet." She let out a long full breath before bending over to ask for KB's foot, and KB matched her with a long, low sigh of her own.

"No looking back," I heard her say under her breath, as she cleaned and scraped each hoof in turn.

"How was that?" I asked as she was finishing.

"Awesome...and a little scary. I was still afraid that she might turn on me, but I feel great that I didn't look back."

"And she didn't turn on you. You trusted your own judgment and acted on it. You assessed your level of safety in this relationship and made a decision about the action you would take."

During her intake session, Jennifer had spoken a great deal about her inability to keep her children safe, and her failed attempts to leave her dangerously abusive situation. The one thing Jennifer didn't do was to talk about her feelings. She appeared to be detached from how she felt, and it was possible that this numbness was keeping her from doing what needed to be done. Her inability to validate, and act on, her feelings was helping to keep her a victim. At some point, she was going to need to face (and honor) those feelings in order to empower herself to make good decisions. We decided to give her an opportunity to start that process with KB.

Jennifer's first task was to identify how she felt and why she felt it by writing down short feeling statements. For example, "I feel... because..." She agreed to write each statement on a separate Post-It note and put it on the horse. We asked her to place the strongest feelings on KB's face and neck and the less intense feelings further back on her body.

Jennifer was very thoughtful about this exercise and took great care in deciding where to place her feeling statements. This may have been the first time that she was validated for having feelings, let alone being given time to sort through their importance. When she finished, KB was a sight to behold: littered with yellow Post-Its from head to tail.

"How does it feel to see all of your feelings out in the open?" I asked her.

She stood silent for a moment, as if taking in the enormity of the situation. "I had no idea that all those feelings were in there. I'm amazed that they all fit inside me and looking at them makes them seem very real, almost too real. Can I just stuff them all back in?" she said, with a quirky smile. I suspected there was some seriousness to her request, however.

"I'm sure you could and that seems to be a comfort zone for you in a way. Let's say that you were going to observe them for a while. How far away from them would you need to be to feel safe?"

"Far," she said without hesitation.

"Well, we have this whole arena."

I asked her to create a distance between herself and KB to give us a picture of how removed she needed to be from her feelings in order to feel safe.

She didn't have to think long before she began walking KB to the far corner of the arena. She placed the horse firmly in the corner and started to walk away.

"I'm going to need to be all the way on the other end," she said, laughing tentatively. Unfortunately, her laughter didn't last long.

Over the years we had learned to expect our horses to behave uncharacteristically in response to clients' needs and that's exactly what KB ended up doing to help Jennifer. As I mentioned in the last chapter, KB was the kind of horse who was happy to sleep her way through a session. She was that horse who liked to "fly under the radar" and in her stoic, trance-like stance she seemed to be saying, "If I stand still long enough, maybe they'll forget I'm here." But not today.

Jennifer only made it a few steps from KB before the horse started to follow her. The image of a woman walking away being followed by a moving mass of Post-It notes was at once comical and poignant. Jennifer must have felt KB's nearness because she glanced around just in time to see the horse, in all her Post-It glory, gaining on her. Jennifer quickened her step. So did KB.

"It looks like it might not be as easy to separate yourself from your feelings as you had hoped," I said.

Jennifer's eyes began to show signs of fear and she picked up a jog. So did KB. Jennifer went into a full run. So did KB.

"As much as you want to escape these feelings, they stay with you," I said. Now Jennifer was running so fast, that I had to run to keep up with her. And KB was relentless.

"I don't like this," she said, and tears began streaming down her face as KB's nose became even with her shoulder.

"What do you need?" I asked, now just a bit breathless.

"I need KB to back off!"

"Why?"

"I'm afraid!"

I pressed her a little here. "Are you afraid of KB or your feelings?"

"Both! Please make her stop!"

"It's time for you to own your own power, Jennifer. I can't rescue you from this. What do you want her to do? What do you want your feelings to do?"

"Get out of my space."

"Then tell her. Tell them, and mean it."

What happened next was as much a surprise to me as it was for Jennifer. She abruptly turned to face KB and with what must have been all the courage she owned, she screamed, "Get away from me! Get the hell out of my space! Get out of my head! Leave me alone!"

And, as if by magic, the twelve hundred pound mass of Post-It note feelings came to a screeching halt, just inches from Jennifer's nose. The sobs that came convulsively now were about release, relief, and redemption.

"Oh my God," she said. "I did it...I really did it."

"What did you do?"

"I stood up for myself. I really did it."

"Yes, you did. You can't outrun your feelings, Jennifer, but you can get control over them. You don't have to allow them to run you over, and you don't have to feel powerless in their presence. You have the power to decide when and how you deal with them."

KB had now, as if by magic, returned to her normal self. No longer possessed, she stood stock still three inches in front of Jennifer, as if sleeping.

"What is your take-away from this experience?" I asked.

Jennifer sat with this question for some time. "She helped me see that I can't outrun my feelings."

"And I wonder if trying to get away from them has only served to frustrate, frighten, and exhaust you?"

She nodded in agreement.

"The fact that you have been courageous enough to place them where they can be observed is a great start, and you've proven that you can stand up to them."

Jennifer was obviously spent. She was hanging on to KB's neck. "May I spend a few minutes saying thank you to her?" she asked.

"Of course," I said. As I watched the pair walk away from me, I wanted to believe that both KB and Jennifer had made a new friend that day.

KB had carried Jennifer's feelings for her, and she had demonstrated the reality that no matter how fast we run, our feelings will always be looming over us, waiting to be dealt with. KB helped Jennifer realize that she had to stand and face her feelings in order to feel in control. This horse had done something that I (with all that training) couldn't do. She had opened a therapeutic door that only she could have opened. Only through the wisdom of this horse were we able to keep the pressure on in just the right measure.

Now it was time for Jennifer to carry her feelings herself, and over the course of the next few sessions, she was able to learn how to do just that. By doing so, she enabled herself to move out of a victim stance and into a place of empowerment.

Jennifer had a total of ten sessions with KB. By the end of her treatment, she was riding bareback without a bridal, and her confidence and joy were undeniable. She learned to trust her judgment, confront her fears, and allow herself to feel joy. Jennifer and her children entered safe housing and received help in leaving the abuse behind. She got a job to support her children and made a new life for herself. I still see her every now and then behind the counter of one of my favorite retail stores.

Thank you, KB, for helping Jennifer see what she needed to see. Thank you, Jennifer, for showing us what real courage looks like.

Part II

Stories of Women and Their Horses

To all the horses in our lives who have helped us find the road to self, and to the women who have courageously shared their stories.

CHAPTER VI

An Unexpected Dream

The Story of Amanda and Chester

Women have love affairs with horses. We kiss
their warm soft noses and trim their quivering
whiskers. We brush them and plait them and paint
their hooves with shiny oil. We bathe them and rub
them and rug them and buy matching accessories
for them.

—Lucy Cavendish, UK News

As much as they love their families, friends, and partners, horsewomen often tell me that it was a horse who was the greatest love of their life. This was certainly true for eleven-year-old Amanda and her horse, Chester.

Chester was a brown Arabian with a black mane and tail and a little star on his forehead. But it wasn't his looks or pedigree that drew Amanda to him. In fact, it was something much less tangible. It was that "something" we feel when we meet someone special. It was that hard-to-describe instant attraction that defies articulation. It was a heart thing.

But Amanda wasn't like some pre-adolescent girls who are obsessed with the dream of owning a horse. In fact, before she met Chester, horses were barely on her radar. She mostly considered them as a factor in her relationship with her grandfather, who was the only horseperson she knew.

Amanda's passions centered around her athleticism, and she was quite happy focusing on sports and being the popular daughter of a small town's school principal. She knew who she was, and she knew how to fit in. Had it not been for an abrupt change in her family's circumstances, it is possible that Amanda would have spent most of her school age years in this safe and stable small-town bubble.

But change happens, whether we want it or not, and Amanda's small-town security was turned upside down when her parents decided to move the family to the country. For them, it meant a new and exciting change; for Amanda, it meant leaving everything she'd ever known. She felt blindsided, and despite her parents' best efforts, she was thrown into a tailspin of trepidation; fearful of losing herself in a new and unpredictable world. So, as it turns out, the path that led her to Chester wasn't one strewn with dreams. It was one of upheaval and uncertainty.

Amanda soon found her neighborhood of close friends replaced with a neighborhood full of farm animals. But the resilience of youth is a powerful thing, and she was soon looking for things to fill her time in a new and foreign place. She didn't look long before an offer to take riding lessons crossed her path and she jumped at the chance; mostly to fill some lonely hours. But she had no idea that this seemingly superficial attempt to pass the time was leading her straight to the horse who would change her life. Straight to the horse who would, surprisingly, be the stuff that little girls' dreams are made of.

If you can have love at first sight with a horse (and I think you can), Amanda and Chester were the perfect example. There was an intimate exchange of energy between the two of them that made her feel safe; like she was at home. Chester became her primary lesson partner, and Amanda became immersed in everything horse. As with most girls who bond with a horse, it didn't take too long before she was dreaming of having him all to herself.

Eleven-year-old girls don't bother worrying about the logistics when it comes to dreaming. It didn't matter that Chester was not for sale; it only mattered that she loved him and that he loved her back. There was no doubt in her mind that she was getting this horse. Period. And she was right.

The addition of Chester to her family kicked life off to a new and exciting start. Almost overnight, Amanda had a purpose and a growing sense of a new way of being. Every morning, she would rush out the door to take care of his every need, and you could hear her yelling, "Good morning, Chester…I love you!"

It looked as though Amanda had come full circle from the confident, happy small-town child to a confident, happy child with an expanded identity. And for a young girl who was feeling the pains of transition, having Chester was everything. It meant that she would no longer be alone or lonely. Chester was her new best friend and, as best friends do, they spent every possible moment together, sharing all the joys and challenges of daily life. Everything they did spoke to the fact that Chester was her one and only, her baby.

Amanda saw Chester not only as her personal savior, but as a blessing for the entire family. He worked his way into their hearts and became a catalyst for helping them overcome the challenges of their transition. Caring for Chester as a team created a new focus that reunited the family through hard work, problem-solving, and humor.

In fact, injecting humor into their lives was one of Chester's fortes. You could fill a book with the lighthearted antics that gave him a reputation as the go-to source for family entertainment. It's hard not to laugh at a horse who breaks out in the middle of the night to steal garden veggies, only to put himself back by morning; or peeks in the kitchen window just to acknowledge that it's breakfast time. Chester was quirky, funny, beautiful, and perfect.

But perfect or not, life with Chester wasn't always easy. Although the difficult moments with him were rare, he did have a knack for occasionally challenging Amanda to dig deep; encouraging her to look at herself with renewed perspective at just the right times.

Like most horses, Chester was like a mirror, providing an unbiased reflection of everything she did in relation to him. His nonjudgmental, yet accurate, feedback encouraged Amanda to see her behaviors as they truly were. It was a testament to the strength of their relationship that Amanda had the courage to look in that mirror. More importantly, she had a keen insight and an ability to translate those challenges into life lessons. They became poignant reminders that having Chester in her life was always in her best interest.

One such reminder happened after a particularly bad training session. Instead of being the compliant partner that Amanda had grown used to, Chester was serving up a plate of disobedience with a side of stubborn. As young, inexperienced horse people usually do, Amanda took her horse's behavior personally. She felt embarrassed, disappointed, and angry; believing that Chester had kept her from achieving what she had set out to do. She was overwhelmed and found herself spanking him and loudly admonishing him, while unbeknownst to her, her trainer watched from the sidelines. The trainer not only told Amanda's mother but cautioned her that if she ever repeated it, Chester would be taken away.

Although Amanda didn't perceive her physical contact with Chester as abusive, it was a real eye-opener, nonetheless. Her knee-jerk reaction to Chester's behavior had put her fully in touch with her conscience and the difficult feelings of shame, regret, and humiliation. She was called on to fully own her actions and to look at the motivations behind them. For this young girl, that day felt like the end of the world. For the first time, she became fully aware of how her competitiveness could come between herself and someone that she dearly loved. It was a big lesson and she never forgot it.

Despite their occasional differences, Amanda genuinely enjoyed involving Chester in her competitive pursuits, and they became a successful team in the show ring, excelling in almost every class in which they chose to show. All classes, that is, except for trail competition. Chester's refusal to take part in this competition was the beginning of Amanda's second life lesson.

Amanda loved this class, and it was an understatement to say that Chester didn't. Because he had inexplicable fears of "stuff," Chester had a great deal of difficulty keeping himself in line during trail competition. That quirkiness Amanda usually loved so much wasn't as much fun when he was dodging mailboxes and refusing water crossings.

But Chester's reluctance only fueled Amanda's desire to overcome. She was determined to convince him that he could manage the course so that she could compete. She created a mock trail setting and jumped on bareback to show him how it was done. Unfortunately, Chester had other plans. Before she knew it, she found herself on the ground, with Chester's head resting softly in her lap. It was as if to say, "I love you, friend, but I have my limits."

This was another opportunity for Amanda to look deeply into her choices. Should she show Chester who was boss and force him to comply so that she could fulfill her desire to compete; or should she open her heart to what he was trying to tell her?

This was a pivotal moment in Amanda's adolescence. It was the moment that she recognized how important it is to consider someone's needs other than her own, and it was a much bigger life lesson than simply acquiescing to her horse's behavior. This moment had an overarching message about relationships and the need for give and take. Chester had once again provided an opportunity for Amanda to step through a portal of personal growth, and once again, she was able to follow his lead.

These are but two of the many lessons about life, love, and relationship that Chester brought to Amanda's life. During their years together, there were many opportunities for them to grow and learn in ways that benefitted them both. But as with most things, it wasn't destined to last forever. During her freshman year in college, Amanda unexpectedly said goodbye to her beloved Chester after he passed away during a routine veterinary treatment.

Amanda was consumed with the grief and sadness that comes with the loss of someone held so dear. She had lost her soulmate, her best friend, and the first true love she'd known outside of her family. Life with Chester had opened Amanda's heart to its fullest capacity. But his untimely and unnecessary death had wounded her so deeply that she vowed never to love so intensely again.

And so it seems that, even in his passing, Chester had left Amanda with one more challenge: to solve the dilemma of how we dare to love so completely, knowing that we may have to experience the deep pain of loss.

Amanda was right: Chester was perfect. He was the perfect example of how horses help us grow, change, and heal by simply living in authentic relationship with them. Thank you, Amanda, for sharing your love story; and thank you, Chester, for showing Amanda how to navigate the challenges of life and what it feels like to love someone with your whole heart.

CHAPTER VII

A Pistol by Another Name

The Story of Christie and Testigo

From horses we may learn not only about the
horse itself but... indeed about ourselves and about
life as a whole.
　　　　　　　　　—George Gaylord Simpson

S ome horses come into our lives like fantasies—to fulfill the
dream of having an in-your-pocket, loves-you-all-the-time best
friend. These are the horses who are our confidants and soul
mates, the yin to our yang. They nuzzle our chests, listen to our
deepest thoughts, and become some of our most cherished moments.
They are our friends in the best sense of the word.

And then there are the horses who enter our lives as antagonists.
Their purpose is to challenge our fortitude and courage. With these
horses, each day brings new opportunities to test the strength of our
equestrian fiber. Our relationship with them becomes a battle of wills
that deflates our confidence and leaves us wondering how we ever
thought we knew anything.

Christie was a thirty-seven-year-old woman who had been
around horses most of her life. She had become a confident equestrian
by riding other people's horses and had waited many years for her
life to flow into a place where having a horse of her own made sense.
Simbad, a black, gentle-spirited Paso Fino, was the horse who helped

her take the step into ownership. He was the first kind of horse; a quintessential feel-good horse, who was a bit like a nurturing parent.

All riders, if they are totally honest, have at least one area of insecurity. But Christie didn't have to address much of her equestrian baggage with Simbad. When her riding skills were "almost there," it was good enough for him. She never needed to dig deep and challenge herself because Simbad was there to fill in the gaps.

Christie had always had an ability to connect with horses at a deeper level, but she did not just connect with Simbad; she let him into her soul. Unfortunately, Simbad was destined to be in Christie's life for only a short time, and she lost him to colic three years after he came to her. She had lost her best friend, and his passing left an indelible impression on her heart.

It took Christie nearly a year to heal, but eventually she began to look for a new equine partner. No one could fill Simbad's shoes, but she gradually felt ready to feel that kind of connection again. Simbad had shown Christie how rewarding life with a Paso Fino could be. If she were going to give her heart to another horse, it could only be a Paso Fino.

Every horse she looked at was fantastic, but there was one horse that outshined them all. He carried himself as if he were a prince, and his black flowing mane gracefully cascaded over his dark bay, nearly perfect conformation. He stood with a countenance that made him appear much larger than his 14.3 stature, and with every stride, he told a story of how amazing he was.

This horse was Testigo, or more formally, Testigo de Besilu, who had come from a renowned Columbian horse farm. He was thoroughly trained and one of the most beautiful horses Christie had ever seen. Just looking at him began to fill her heart with romantic visions of what their lives would be like if lived together.

Testigo virtually glittered, and Christie was blinded by the sparkle. He was like a beautiful, shiny button that made her forget everything except what it would feel like to ride such a magnificent animal. She could see herself sitting astride his wide shoulders, riding his perfect gait, and basking in the pride of ownership. She envisioned them riding down the street amidst the envious scrutiny of observers.

It was love at first sight, and she hoped he would be the horse to fill the void of her beloved Simbad.

Initially, Christie was on an emotional high. She could not believe that she owned a horse like Testigo. But as they began to settle into their lives together, she realized that her shiny button was more like a bedazzled Colt 45. This horse was not going to be another version of Simbad. This was going to be the horse who would challenge her to her core.

It is not that Testigo was a bad horse; that was far from the truth. In fact, he was highly trained and incredibly smart. But he was proving to be the antithesis of what Christie had originally set out to find. When his bells and whistles gave way to challenging behaviors, Christie used her highly developed intuition to look deep into who he was. She saw a horse that was full of attitude and had all the traits of human narcissism. He demanded perfect communication from a perfect rider and had little room for forgiveness. Worst of all, Christie sensed that Testigo knew he was tapping into her weaknesses, and she had the impression that he found a bit of humor in his ability to do so.

The challenges to Christie's deepest insecurities began almost immediately, as she found herself tested at every turn. Riding Testigo was as much a mental game as it was a physical one, and he repeatedly let her know that he could (and would) win at both. She was used to riding horses that did what they were told. She was used to Simbad, who always did the right thing by her. Not only did Testigo fail to do what was asked of him, he tested her horsemanship in ways that it had never been tested before.

Testigo was a horse who had an immense amount of pride and if challenged, had a lot of pushback. It was that pushback that Christie was most afraid of. Not knowing how far he would go to stay in charge began to stifle her ability to lead. She could feel her confidence and faith in her ability being eroded, and she was left frozen by the fear of not knowing just how far he would take his obsession with winning. She often found herself in situations in which her fear of what he might do stopped her from doing what she knew she should do.

For a medium-sized horse, Testigo had a lot of brio, which is typical for the Paso Fino. They are known for having a mixture of energy, arrogance, and fire that is tempered only by a willingness to be taught and controlled. Testigo had the first two in abundance but was likely absent when they doled out the willingness to be dominated. Christie was afraid that if she let him experience the full extent of his personality, things would get out of control. She could feel Testigo slowly chipping away at her confidence, and she was doubting her ability to rise to the challenges he was presenting.

Testigo was nothing like Simbad, and he was not soul mate material—at least not yet. However, Testigo was still the horse she wanted to look at. He was still the horse she wanted to ride and to be seen riding. She still thought he was phenomenal, and her desire to feel phenomenal when she was with him kept her in the game.

Although she could not articulate it, something told her that this horse was supposed to be in her life. She could not and would not give up. She knew this meant digging deep: deep into who he was and deep into who she wanted to be when she was with him.

Christie knew that Testigo was not your run-of-the-mill ornery horse, and she saw his protests as a matter of honor.

She had the sense that, for Testigo, totally giving up control was akin to losing his soul. The need to protect his honor ran deep, and he left the impression that he would fight to the death before giving it up. She had seen him lay himself down more than once, rather than give in to control for control's sake.

However, helping Testigo unravel this deep-seated issue was complicated. It was becoming apparent that in order to help Testigo, Christie was first going to have to unravel some things about herself. She desperately wanted to show off her shiny button, but she needed to address the glaring issues between them as well.

Testigo came with an inflexible need to protect himself. Christie came with old insecurities that she hadn't worked through and leadership skills that were yet to be fully developed. Testigo's baggage caused him to put her on notice: he wouldn't be man-handled into submission. Until she addressed her insecurities, she would be left not knowing how to respond to the line he was drawing in the sand.

Despite her fears (or maybe because of them), Christie's desire to show him off to the world outweighed her lack of confidence, and she ventured into the show ring, perhaps a bit prematurely, hoping that it would all work itself out there. She hired a good trainer and launched Testigo into the show circle. But he wasn't going to make it easy for her. Before succeeding in any arena, she was going to have to earn his respect, which was something she had yet to do.

Christie soon discovered that trouble almost always followed when Testigo sensed that the rider wasn't focused, on-point, and in complete unison. Christie was a good rider, but there were elements of her riding that she had not yet perfected, and Testigo was not the kind of horse who wanted to wait around for her to get her stuff together. He was a little like the poet Horace: waiting to seize the day. Or in his case, to seize the moment when he first sensed her falling into insecure ground. He would latch onto the realization that he was in control and run with it (sometimes literally) before Christie could figure out how to pull the moment together.

Because of their inability to become one as horse and rider, their early days in the show ring were strewn with embarrassing and frightening episodes. Christie never knew when Testigo would stage an all-out refusal, when he would take issue with other horses, or when he would simply assert his own agenda. These moments became so predictable that Christie found herself automatically anticipating the worst.

Each time they entered the arena, her thoughts would race toward her fears. She was afraid of her horse, yes, but she was also afraid that the people she wanted to impress would be judging her. She was afraid that she could not live up to her own, or others', expectations. As she imagined all the ways in which this horse was about to test her, she would forget to breathe, and the panic would rise out of the knot in her stomach. As she anticipated the embarrassment of failing, she could almost see her ability to lead lying inert on the arena floor.

With each successive showing experience, she worked herself into the same mental twist. She knew she was digging herself a hole, and Testigo knew it too. With a high-energy horse like Testigo, Christie sensed that all these factors could someday come together to create the perfect storm. Even though he had never hurt her, he had learned to huff and puff sufficiently to leave her guessing about the extent to which he would take it. She even began to feel as if it was all a joke to him. Christie could feel their relationship deteriorating, and her resolve to make it work began to wear thin.

Things consistently got worse and being with Testigo became a daily test of her mettle. Almost everything turned into an argument. Even a simple catch and halter could dissolve into a battle of the wills. Being with Testigo left her chronically frustrated, angry, and fearful: three emotions that will almost always leave the rider throwing in the towel, and the horse with the upper hand.

Christie increasingly felt the pain of her ineffectiveness in correcting his behaviors. This was not the horsewoman she knew herself to be. Her compassion and levelheadedness were being replaced with full-tilt exasperation, and her frustration with Testigo began to erode at the fiber of their relationship.

Most of the time, she felt disconnected, powerless, and out of control. Nevertheless, something at her core said that she still wanted to be the perfect rider that made their picture complete.

While the issues between the two of them were coming to a head, Christie was becoming aware that the themes playing out between them were also (almost serendipitously) playing out in other areas of her life. She was having similar issues with foster children and trying to run a successful business with difficult partners. It seemed that everywhere she turned, she was being met with resistance and pushback from those in her closest circles. It was as if her life with Testigo was mirroring her life outside the barn. Instead of the barn being a place of solace and healing, it was becoming just one more rendition of what she was experiencing everywhere else.

Out of a desperate need to make it work, and a deep commitment that she felt toward all animals, Christie finally made the decision to temporarily relocate Testigo to her mother's ranch. This would give her time to do her own soul-searching and determine once and for all whether the two of them could make a go of it.

But the hardest part of her journey came after Testigo left. Christie knew in her heart that the trouble in their relationship wasn't

Testigo's fault. The fact that her relationship with him mirrored other relationships in her life told her that it was she who would need to make most of the initial changes.

Christie was determined to look objectively into the changes she'd need to make. Taking ownership of her need for personal change was a step that required a great deal of courage and honesty. A person of lesser courage and commitment might have simply admitted failure or blamed the horse. Someone else might have rehomed a horse that was challenging them far beyond their zone of personal comfort. Certainly, no one would have blamed her if that were the road she took.

But taking the easy way out had never been in Christie's makeup. She opted to spend their time apart looking deep within her own psyche and asking that pivotal question: could she dig down deep enough to overcome the fear that she had allowed to dominate their life together? She knew that, without this core change, they would never make it.

It turned out that the time away from Testigo was exactly what she needed. It gave her the chance to reconnect with the feelings of love and commitment that were still alive deep in her heart. After a long period of renewed self-awareness and exploring her bottom line, she realized that it wasn't just a sense of commitment that obliged her to keep going. At her core, she really loved him, and giving up was not an option.

But how was she going to take back the control she had lost and still honor who Testigo was at his core? She wasn't sure how she was going to accomplish that, but she knew that she had a twofold starting point: She would need to address the origins of her insecurities, and she would need to learn to let go of her need for outside approval. She would need to accept that temporary failures could be a path to ultimate success. Finally, she would need to find a training strategy that would help her muster up the courage to lead in a way that could connect with Testigo's sensitivities.

Testigo's serendipitous entrance into Christie's life was taking her on a self-imposed journey to her core; and as if to round out the serendipitous energy, she was introduced to the training methods of natural horsemanship. It was exactly what she needed when she needed it. Natural Horsemanship is a training philosophy that works with a horse's natural instincts and teaches people how to communicate with them in a way that fosters respect, trust, and understanding. The tenets of natural horsemanship gave her permission to start over, and for the first time, she felt a glimmer of hope.

She brought Testigo home with newfound energy and quickly realized that this new method of interacting was exactly what they both needed. But it wasn't always smooth sailing, especially in the beginning. Christie needed to learn how to drop old habits that did not work and to ask for help when she needed it. She was developing a can-do attitude, and the better she got at the art of negotiation, the more Testigo began to meet her halfway.

Christie was starting to enjoy their time together, and it was obvious that Testigo could feel the positive feelings that she brought to their workouts. His rebellious antics began to subside, and Christie's fear and anger were replaced with a quiet resolve and clear communication. She had learned that everything wasn't about getting what she wanted, and she was successfully teaching Testigo that it wasn't all about him either.

She felt her confidence growing daily, and soon Christie was getting what she wanted more of the time. She was leading with confidence and compassion, and Testigo was dropping his need to "fight to the death." It was turning into something fantastic.

Christie learned how to create relationship by asking the right questions. For the first time, Christie was beginning to see things from the perspective of fostering growth; for herself and for Testigo. It was no longer about who won and who didn't. It was about how to win as a team.

Christie and Testigo are still together today, and Testigo has taught Christie much about herself, about the benefits of patience, and the power of negotiation. They both learned how to adopt a win-win attitude and to partner up toward the same goals.

New training methods did not change who Testigo was, but then they were not designed to. She will always honor his right to be who he is, including that part of him that wants to see how far he can take a challenge. The difference is that, now, Christie knows exactly what to do. She has developed a relationship of trust and is confident that she and Testigo will always find a way to meet in the middle. And while these are great mottos for horsemanship, they are also fantastic metaphors for life itself.

All the relationship changes she was making with Testigo extended far outside the two of them. Her life experiences, especially those with her foster children and business partners, were improving as well. Listening to Testigo was teaching her how to become an assertive and benevolent leader in all aspects of her life.

Christie often tells Testigo how much she appreciates the special kind of gift he brought into her life. She thanks him for helping her take an honest look at herself, for challenging her to become the skilled rider that she is today, and for showing her what it's like to be truly authentic. He gave her exactly what she needed when she needed it, and that takes a special kind of heartfelt wisdom.

The miraculous thing is that, whether our horses are soul mates or antagonists, they can bring powerful learning and growth into our lives. Thank you, Simbad, for giving Christie her soul mate. Thank you, Testigo, for bringing the kind of challenge into her life that would show her the strength of her fiber, carry her ever further on her equestrian journey, and teach her that love that sprouts from antagonism can be just as deep and rewarding as any other kind.

CHAPTER VIII

God Speaks Through All Things

The Story of Tawnya and Izabelle

*Be strong when you are weak, be brave when
you are scared, be humble when you are victorious.*
—Michelle Moschetti

orses put us in touch with who we truly are. And for those of us who can stay silent long enough, they can put us in touch with our innermost being. Some would even say that our experiences with them have a direct link to our relationship with God.

Tawnya didn't need a horse to remind her of her connection to God. She was a woman who found God in every aspect of life. But she was about to learn that even those who are deeply connected to their faith can become closer to God through sharing an experience with a horse.

Tawnya was first introduced to the magic of horses in her work with The EMBRACE Equine Ministry Program in Athol, Idaho. It was through this program that she witnessed many small miracles that came as a result of pairing horses with troubled youth. She saw them help to transform the minds, hearts, and behaviors of almost every child they worked with. In their own way, these horses helped teens open their hearts to conversations about self, life, and God.

Although Tawnya didn't have experience with horses, the women she worked with did. It didn't take long for her to understand that it wasn't only troubled teens that benefitted from knowing these animals. She also observed the strong connection these women had to their own horses. Just by being in relationship with them, the women were graced with metaphors for life, relationships and spirituality.

The women of the EMBRACE team were making plans for their first annual ride into the Montana backcountry. Tawnya listened to the women as they talked about their hopes that this trip would be the first of many rewarding trips together. They seemed excited about sharing experiences that would bring them closer to each other and closer to God. She could tell that this trip held much more meaning for the EMBRACE team than a casual ride in the mountains.

Tawnya wanted to experience all the things her friends were talking about. But when it came to riding, she was a newbie in the strictest sense of the word. Her knowledge of horses could fit in a thimble with room to spare. But her desire to commune with nature, her friends, and God, eventually outweighed the fact that she didn't know a pommel from a cantle or a cinch from a breastplate. Her friends convinced her that they could get her ready enough to join them on their trip. Truth be told, she really didn't need much convincing. She wanted to be a part of the scenario they were painting of horses, nature, camaraderie, and God.

As her friends rallied around to teach her horsemanship 101, Tawnya's spiritual journey with Isabelle or "Izzy" officially began. Izzy seemed the perfect match for her. She was an eight-year-old bay quarter horse who was a strong and capable veteran of the backcountry. It probably didn't hurt that she was the ride most often picked for children and had a reputation for being lazy.

However, as the lessons progressed, Tawnya realized how much there was to learn. She could feel the anxiety taking hold and found herself frequently asking the women if they were sure she could pull this off. And every time she asked, her mentors would tell her that she could do this. Her only job was to stay in the saddle. And she would say, "Okay, show me how."

Tawnya's faith in her friends might have been akin to the faith she often put in God. She recalled that every time she had to face her fears, she would end up taking a leap of faith, knowing that God had her back. This moment, with these women, was the same. She knew that they had her back as she was preparing to take a giant leap of faith.

Almost before she knew it, the trip was in full swing, and her first backcountry ride was ahead of her. It's probably a good thing no one told her that only experienced horse people tend to venture into the rugged backcountry. It's also probably a good thing that no one told her just how rugged, rugged can get, because it wasn't long into the first day's ride before the group was faced with a steep, narrow trail.

Tawnya looked at what seemed to be a pencil-thin line that was flanked by slippery shale on one side and a sheer drop-off on the other. She could see that, once they committed themselves, there would be no turning back.

As they began their single file progression, Tawnya looked over the edge, which was probably her first mistake. Anxiety kicked in almost without warning as she watched her stirrup dangling over thin air. She could feel the fear rise from her belly as she was suddenly struck by a dose of reality. She was on a real horse traversing a real cliff, and she really had no idea what she was doing. If Izzy stumbled, they would simply fall into air. She tried to keep her mind from traveling into the fearful images of free falling toward sure death. She just kept repeating the mantra her friends had given her: "Stay in the saddle, stay in the saddle, stay in the saddle." As they walked along, she tried to console herself by remembering that these thirteen women and their horses had encountered many trails such as this. For them, it was probably old news.

Tawnya had expected an uneventful, if somewhat nerve-racking, first experience. What she hadn't expected was trouble right out of the gate. The women riding ahead of her had stirred up a hornet's nest, and Tawnya was next in line. She could feel the tension mounting in both her friends and the horses. The only thing to do was to get through the swarm as quickly as possible, to minimize the chances of getting stung. But Tawnya knew that a stirred-up hornet is an angry hornet, and a return trip would be much more dangerous.

Since turning around wasn't an option, their only choice was to get through quickly and hope that there would be an alternate way back.

Unfortunately, soon after the last woman cleared the narrow trail, the group ran into multiple downed trees. The main trail was completely blocked and there would be no way out except to double back. They had no option but to face the now ticked-off swarm of hornets again.

To make matters worse, the horses were now aware of the swarm, and Tawnya could feel Izzy's apprehension rising. She was afraid that Izzy was preparing to charge through the massive angry swarm. She had visions of Izzy running uncontrollably across the slippery shale and knew that she had to keep her from doing that. But how? How was she supposed to keep a frightened horse from doing something dangerous? In that moment, she realized just how little she knew and how ill-prepared she was. She felt her fear move into panic as she pulled back on the reins as hard as she could. She had stopped thinking…she was simply reacting. She had such a death grip on Izzy's mouth, that Izzy couldn't walk, much less run.

Something she would learn after the fact is that if you close the door on a frightened horse's ability to move forward, they will find the only way out they know, which is usually straight up. And that's exactly what Izzy did; rearing up so high that her butt hit the ground.

Tawnya could hear all the voices around her yelling instructions. "Give her her head, lean forward, let out the reins, breathe, calm down!" But her sheer panic and her novice horsemanship kept her from understanding the meaning of their words. She had no idea that "letting out the reins" meant to loosen her hold so that Izzy could have the freedom to move. But even if she had understood the words, she would likely have continued to rebel against the idea of giving a panicked horse freedom. She clung to the reins as she felt herself freeze in place.

After what seemed a lifetime, Tawnya heard footsteps running up from behind, but she was too frightened to turn around to see that it was her friend, Becca. Becca was trying to approach the frightened pair but quickly turned back, realizing that trying to reach Izzy and Tawnya would mean increased danger for everyone. She heard the footsteps retreating, and her fear dug in.

Tawnya knew that everyone was trying to help her and that she was surrounded by people who cared for her safety, but she had never felt so afraid. She felt completely alone, trying to save herself from a problem that she had no idea how to solve.

Blind panic was settling in. She couldn't focus, couldn't follow directions, and everything felt surreal. How could this be happening to her? Were she and Izzy going to slip over the edge into certain death? Just as the worst seemed inevitable, Tanya saw Teri, who had been riding in front of her, get off her horse. She watched Teri methodically try to make her way back to them. Tawnya couldn't believe that Teri would leave her horse and traverse the dangerous hillside to help get her and her horse to safety. Even in her panicked state, Tawnya knew that this woman was putting her own safety at great risk to help her.

The trail was so narrow that Teri couldn't reach the two of them, and she was forced to give directions from a distance. Tawnya watched and listened as Teri tried to demonstrate what to do. Even through her panic, Tawnya realized the wisdom of her friend. Teri was using language that was in Tawnya's frame of reference. She seemed somehow able to see the situation as Tawnya was seeing it and guide her with words and actions that she could understand. Teri told her to lean forward and loosen the reins to stop Izzy from rearing. She said, "Just let her go." She explained that Izzy's innate self-preservation would keep her from running. But Tawnya was not confident that Izzy wouldn't run. After all, she was getting repeatedly being stung by a mass of raging hornets. But finally, Tawnya had no other choice but to trust both her friend and her horse.

Even though she had someone by her side, it was Tawnya who had to make the decision to do the right thing. She was the only one who could muster up the courage to do what she was being guided to do. No one, not her friends, or even God, could rescue her from the responsibility of ultimately doing the right thing and saving herself. God could put the right people in front of her, and those people could support and guide, but it was she who would have to take ultimate responsibility in choosing to comply with their life-saving advice.

Somehow, she pulled herself out of her panic long enough to listen to Teri's words. Putting all her trust in her friend and her mount, Tawnya loosened the reins, leaned forward and prayed. And everything Teri had told her came true. Izzy didn't run away. She used her head and got them both out to safety.

Once Tawnya was able to pull off to a safe spot, she turned to make sure that everyone else was getting out as well. Surprisingly, she saw that all the women were off their horses. *What happened to the mantra, "stay in the saddle no matter what?"* she thought to herself. She had done what everyone told her to do, but they had all done something different. Why?

Later that night, as the women settled in, they had a chance to help Tawnya understand their decision. They helped her to see that experience really is the best teacher.

Tawnya understood their point, but she wondered if they knew that she really thought she was going to die up there. It would have been easy to slip into thinking that they were making light of this harrowing experience. But then her memory flashed to the sounds and images of Becca and Teri risking their own lives to help her. The images flooded her mind and heart, and she felt a sense of boundless gratitude. No one could ever know exactly how she felt, and that wasn't important. What was important was that they saw a friend in a dangerous place and they rallied to keep her safe.

And then her thoughts turned to Izzy. Largely due to Tawnya's inexperience, Izzy had reared up. But she also realized that, even though Izzy could have easily thrown her, she never did. Izzy was the one who had tried to keep her cool in the face of disaster. In a real sense, Izzy had contributed to saving both of their lives. Despite being guided by a novice rider, Izzy had made the best decisions she could make. She kept her head when everything around her was in chaos.

As Tawnya continued to share her thoughts and feelings, the group's leader, Renae, began to see the spiritual metaphors rise to the surface. She shared her insights with them and likened their experience to the spiritual crises that so many of us experience at some point in our lives. The group played back the events in the order they occurred, and for each event there seemed to be a life metaphor.

On this ride, there had been a line of women; each having to get through the same hornet's nest. Only one could go through at a time. They talked about the way they handled the situation as a group. Each woman had a choice: she could focus only on her own need to get through without getting stung, leaving the others to their own devices, or she could be connected to each rider before and after her, ready to learn from those who went before, and prepared to assist those who were coming up from behind.

Following are Tawnya's words as she describes her experience and Renae's spiritual translation of the day's events:

> Sometimes, as we go through the events in our lives, we are oblivious to what might happen to others who come along behind us. Some of us might not get through so easily. We might get stuck in the thick of it and need help to get out. And then there are the people behind those people who can witness what they are going through, which allows them to prepare. And sometimes, the ones who get through it are compelled to go back and help those who can't free themselves. That really stuck with me for a long time. Because the spiritual meaning of what happened was so much bigger than the event itself. The picture suddenly grew from this singular event to every challenge we, as spiritual beings, experience. Suddenly I was drawn to think about every other time that I had been in the thick of it spiritually and someone came to help me. And I thought about my spiritual obligation to help others who were spiritually stuck.
>
> I realized that I was being called to examine my spiritual choices in times of distress; not just for myself, but for others. If I see the spiritual

freight train coming, do I stand aside and hope the person can get out of its way, or do I stand in front of it with them? Just like Becca, who was behind me and decided not to intervene, I am faced with the decision of whether intervening in someone else's spiritual struggle will help or hinder their progress. And if I decide to help someone in their struggle, I might need to use their spiritual reference points instead of my own; changing how I communicate so that they can accept my help.

The group felt called to not only look at what it means to be a spiritual guide for someone else but what it means for the one being guided. Tawnya had been in a situation in which she had to choose whether to listen to the guidance she was getting.

While I was in an all-out panic, I had to pull it together enough to listen to someone who was trying to guide me in something I knew nothing about. Not to mention all the commotion that was going on around me. The people who were trying to help me must have been fearful that they would have to watch Izzy and I go over the side of this mountain. This was a great metaphor for life, because when we get scared, what do we do? We dig in and up the control. We metaphorically tighten up the reins for fear that if we let go, we won't be safe. Letting go when we are in the middle of a panic and trusting other people and trusting God is a really hard thing to do.

For the remainder of the trip, Tawnya was understandably on edge. But her anxiety gradually turned to confidence as she learned to give the reins over to Izzy. She learned when she needed to guide Izzy and when she needed to let her use her own judgement. She realized that Izzy was pretty darn good at filling in the gaps of a new rider. But learning to trust another being (whether it is horse or human) to make the right choices can be a scary thing. In those moments, it is natural to want to tighten the control. With Izzy's help, Tawnya may have learned one of her most important life lessons: when (and how) to let go. Let go and let Izzy, let go and let friends, let go and let God.

What started out as a backcountry adventure ended up being a spiritual lesson that would indelibly be recorded in Tawnya's book of life. She and Izzy remained riding partners for some time, and Tawnya grew to trust and appreciate this levelheaded soul.

Thank you, Izzy, for being present when Tawnya could not, for being of sound mind in the middle of chaos, and for giving Tawnya an experience that she will take with her for the rest of her life.

Part III

Take the Journey to Self, and Let a Horse Lead You There

To Lodur, Deramie, Skjoni, Riley, Legend and Chance for showing me the way to myself.

CHAPTER IX

Deramie's Gift: Part I

A horse doesn't care how much you know until
he knows how much you care.
                                                        —Pat Parelli

T he journey toward an equine-assisted psychotherapy program began the moment I realized that my childhood, and
much of my adult life, had been tainted with the message
that I was not good enough.

It was a horse named Deramie who first helped me shed light
on this falsehood I had carried around for so many years. She was the
horse who introduced me to the healing power of horse-human relationships. It was because of her that I began to understand myself.
And it was the emotional, tumultuous, and ultimately rewarding
relationship I had with her that gave me insight into how horses
could help to heal a broken human spirit.

I offer this story, not only as a testament to the power of the
horse-human relationship, but as an example of the fantastic ripple
effect that emerged as a result of the relationship between just one
human and one horse.

As a way of beginning, let me start with a personal disclosure:
I don't do blood. At least I didn't until I found my horse standing in
a pool of it. I had arrived home to find Deramie standing at the far
corner of the arena, blood spitting out of a vein in her neck.

She was a beautiful black Arabian/Quarter horse who had come
to us after being left on her own without human or herd to help her

pass the time. She had just enough attitude to make her intimidating, but not enough to render her dangerous.

I was a forty-one-year-old cowgirl wannabe who, among other things, was easily intimidated. Good match.

This was a day I would never forget. It was the day that would begin a journey into the core of my being. It was a day that would start a series of perceptual insights that would turn relationships, as I knew them, upside down. More important, it was the planted seed that would eventually sprout into a tree of clinical pursuits, ending in the establishment of an equine-assisted therapy program. In short, this horse was about to change my life. But I had to help save hers first.

The vet's visit confirmed that she had been impaled by a T-post. "The hole is so jagged that I don't even know if I can suture it up," he said. "You're going to want to get covers on those posts if you don't want this to happen again." He gave the instructions with a tone that was absent of inflection, and most people might not have heard the hint of judgment behind the words. But I did.

I don't think I was aware of the feeling in the pit of my stomach that told me I wasn't good enough nor was I in touch with the history that had caused me to develop a keen ability to pick up on the subtlest of gestures. The only thing I could have told you then was that my horse was bleeding to death, the vet thought I was an idiot, and it would be my fault if she died. I felt stupid and guilty.

I had let her down, and I could hardly bring myself to breathe without tears. If Deramie died, the buck would stop with me...the idiot-child who didn't know enough to cover a t-post. I swallowed hard to keep the lump in my throat from erupting.

The vet's fingers raced to beat the blood to the opening of the wound, as he deftly sutured what little skin was available. The sound of his voice brought me out of my guilt-ridden stupor. "I need another set of hands. Can you just hold these two sides together, so that I can get the needle through without tearing?"

Did I mention that I was completely neurotic when it came to blood? The first step in this journey seemed to be that I was going to have to put my fears aside in order to help someone else. I'm ashamed to say that this was not something I'd ever had to do. As the youngest child of three, I had always been protected from having to go too far out of my comfort zone. If I was afraid, someone else would do it. If I was tired, someone else would take over. This was the first time that I remember having to buck up and get 'er done. So, heart pounding, I tried to master the art of assisting without looking.

An hour later, the vet and I were wrapping up. He bathed the wound and administered another sedative. Although dog-tired and emotionally drained, we were both relieved that she had come through this part of the ordeal.

"This is makeshift at best," he cautioned. "There's a real chance that infection has already set in and the sutures might not hold. If we are going to keep it from getting worse, she'll have to have the wound cleaned out several times a day. I've had to leave a big part of it open, so you'll probably start to see pus-like drainage. It's important that you clean that out thoroughly every time."

I might also have neglected to mention that I don't do pus. All my life, I diligently tried to stay away from anything sick, dead, dying, disgusting, or smelly.

For all those reasons, I was having a hard time holding it together. I found myself flashing back to second grade, when Timmy Wilder ate paste and threw it up all over my desk. I'd spent the rest of the day quite sure that I was about to throw up as well. That's how I felt now. It was Deramie who was aching and feverish, but I felt sick and couldn't stop shivering. It was as if I too had been injured and was developing a fever. Just like I'd obsessed over the fear that I'd throw up Timmy Wilder's paste, I couldn't stop thinking about how awful it would be to feel like Deramie must be feeling now. As I looked at my beautiful horse, all I could think of was that she might die because I was stupid.

The vet dutifully warned me that Deramie was not out of the woods and that she would need constant attention for the next few weeks. Cleaning her wound would be painful, and he cautioned that she might be difficult to handle. Great. He instructed me to check on her every few hours through the night and to call him if she took a turn for the worse.

Two repetitive thoughts were running through my mind: Deramie could be a bitch even when she felt good, and I would have to overcome multiple neurotic tendencies in order to see this through. I'd have to set aside my fear of her, my fear of disgusting things, and my fear of death in order to take care of her. But at the end of the day, I was all she had. The weight of that reality bore down on me like nothing I'd felt before.

I couldn't bring myself to leave her for quite some time. I stroked her neck and talked to her softly until I could feel the weight of her head pressing on my shoulder, telling me that she had fallen asleep.

CHAPTER X

Deramie's Gift: Part II

Being deeply loved by someone gives you strength,
while loving someone deeply gives you courage.
—Author Unknown

T he next morning arrived on the heels of a sleepless, fearful night. My heart was in my throat as I approached the barn with a bucket of warm water, a sterilized cloth, and cleaning solution. The thought that I was about to go head-to-head with a bloody pus-filled gaping hole on a cranky horse had me weak in the knees. This was not one of my shining moments.

I don't remember how long I stood there, but once I got down to business, something inside me shifted. I stopped thinking about my own fears and discomfort and was able to attend to the task at hand. Deramie seemed to know that I was there to help and was uncharacteristically amiable. Her choice to allow me to care for her gave me the opportunity to find a strength within; one that I could not have found if I were battling a severe case of the cranks from her.

This was the story for the next three weeks. Little by little, I started to feel my confidence grow. I was developing a can-do atti-tude instead of a fear-based avoidance. Wound cleanings three times a day and extended periods of time together were solidifying the bond between us, and I was beginning to feel that a true partnership was emerging. I was beginning to trust her, and I believed that she was beginning to trust and love me. I believed that she felt gratitude for the sacrifices I was making on her behalf, and that this was bringing us closer. That, by the way, is something animal owners are good at—assigning human feelings and motives to their pets.

And then came the light bulb moment. As I opened her stall door on the last day of our wound washing regimen, I was eager to see my girl and to go through our bonding ritual. But as I stepped into her space, I was greeted not by the loving, grateful horse who had amiably allowed me to nurse her back to health. I was greeted by the old cranky Deramie on steroids. With her head down and her ears pinned, she pawed the ground as if to challenge my right to be in her space at all.

All my insecurities came rushing back, and I immediately turned and bolted out of the stall. All the courage and warm, fuzzy feelings that I thought I had developed were suddenly gone. But what surprised me the most were the thoughts and feelings that took their place.

I remember the feeling of betrayal I felt and the anger that rose into my throat as I stood safely outside her stall, spewing accusations and blame at her. And I remember the gut-wrenching sadness that followed so close behind. I had done everything right. I had been there for her, forsaking my own needs. How could she do this to me? I had let down my guard and trusted that she loved me. How could she turn on me? HOW COULD SHE ABANDON ME?

I suddenly realized that the tears and accusations were no longer about Deramie. They were about my mother and the life I had spent trying to heal from the abandonment I felt when she sent me away at six years old. And they were about the fear I felt that others would ultimately turn on me if I didn't do everything in my power to please them. After all, my mother had sent me away because I wasn't good enough, right? I had grown up with the subconscious belief that others would see that I was deficient as well, and they too would "send me away." It was in that moment of utter rejection that I felt about Deramie that the subconscious made its way into the conscious realm. Deramie was now staring at me through the stall door, ears up and eyes wide, and I felt a wave of love and remorse for all the yelling wash over me. I suddenly realized that her behavior wasn't about me at all. It was about her. I didn't cause her to behave that way toward me. She behaved that way because it was the only way she knew to get her point across. She was telling me in the only way she knew that she was over it. Deramie hadn't abandoned me because of something I'd done. She was just trying to save herself. (The vet confirmed later that Deramie had developed a case of depression as part of the aftermath of her trauma.) What followed was a rapid unfolding of the true reasons behind my mother's behavior. Although she did abandon me, she didn't do it because of anything I had done. She did it to save herself, and she did it in response to a severe depression that left her fearful that she could not care for me. Deramie was doing the best she could in the moment to save herself. So had my mother. And I finally felt the freedom of understanding that none of it had anything to do with my worthiness. I opened the stall door with a newfound attitude. I felt compassion for this animal who was doing the best she could to communicate with this wannabe cowgirl. I opened the door wide and watched as she ran past me into the open air and the fresh green spring grass.

Because of her depression, Deramie stood in the corner of the pasture for a week before she began to venture out and become a horse again. I sat with her each day as often as I could to let her know that she was not alone. And I'll never forget the moment when she came to meet me where I sat, touching her nose briefly on my forehead before running off to be herself again.

Thank you, Deramie, for knowing exactly when to be a safe place for me to explore my fears and when to help me challenge the ways I thought about myself and the world. You remain forever in my heart.

CHAPTER XI

Riley

The Journey to a Mustang's Heart

Technique can get to a certain level, but beyond that, connection with the horse's heart is necessary.
—Nuno Oliviera

Mustangs hold a special place in my heart, and for reasons I've never figured out, I began crossing paths with them around 2005. But it wasn't just any mustang I was coming across. Somehow, I kept landing in places where either the horse or their owner needed help. Most of the time, I was being put in touch with friends, or friends of friends, who needed help making first contact with their newly acquired adoptees. Their stories were almost all the same. Even after running their horses around in circles for weeks, they were still unable to approach or halter them.

It only took working with a few mustangs for me to realize that I had an ability to connect with these intelligent, sensitive creatures, and I was developing a serious-sized soft spot in my heart for them. I suddenly wanted to immerse myself in everything mustang and finagled my way into volunteering at local mustang adoptions.

Not long after, I was approached by the Bureau of Land Management. They wondered if I would be willing to work with mustangs who had been abused or neglected. I don't think it was because I was a top-notch trainer (because I wasn't). I think it was because they heard I had enough patience to work with emotionally damaged horses. It took roughly a second for me to accept.

Helping horses separate themselves from abusive memories is part of creating a fresh foundation for their training, and it can take months of hard work to help them get there. But for me, it was like living in Utopia: spending hour upon hour building a foundation of love and trust. Not everyone would agree with me, but I believe that until a trainer has helped a horse unravel an abusive history, they can't adequately train them.

But it wasn't all utopic. As a BLM volunteer, I had to hear about the abuses endured by my foster horses. I needed to know how well-intentioned but inadequate trainers/owners had resorted to tying their horses to poles without food or water to "teach" them submission; or about horses who had been choked down, leaving them gasping for air, in an attempt to catch and halter them.

One such horse was Riley. The BLM had called me out to the home of a woman named…well, let's call her Sarah. She claimed that her mustang was "loco" and wanted someone to come help her fix him.

When I arrived, Sarah brought me to meet her mustang, Riley. What I saw made a lump of sadness form in my throat. Riley was standing knee-deep in mud in a tiny round pen with solid walls. He had no visuals of the outside world and movement was, at best, difficult. His mane was matted to the point that, even from a distance, I could see it pulling at his skin.

Sarah explained that she had owned Riley for several months and was still unable to approach him. Recently, she had resorted to calling in a group of people who called themselves mustang specialists. These "specialists" promised her that they would have her horse haltered in less than an hour.

Many hours later, they had tied Riley to a pole with an extremely short line and no ability to access food or water. Sarah had been told by the people who tied him down that he was incorrigible. They convinced her that his thrashing and falling to the ground was evidence that he was crazy.

The tie down had been so short that when he fell to the ground, the air was choked out of him. He passed out, only to awaken even more distraught. This process apparently went on for quite some time, thrashing until he choked out, then getting up and doing it all over again. Finally, the mustang gurus gave up and went home, leaving Sarah with an emotionally damaged horse who may never trust humans again.

To say that I was appalled, flabbergasted, sickened, and angry doesn't even begin to explain the tumult of emotions that were tearing through my insides. I couldn't fathom that Sarah believed that she and this group of people had no part in creating his current emotional state. A-mazing.

I approached Riley's enclosure, standing at the gate to observe his demeanor. His nostrils were flaring, his head was high, and his eyes were like round, unblinking discs.

"Do you see what I'm talking about?" Sarah said. "He's loco."

"What makes you think he's loco?" I asked.

"Well look at him...his nostrils are flaring and he's snorting."

"He's frightened," I said.

"He's not frightened! He's angry...and crazy...and dangerous."

This horse was scared out of his mind. Just our being at the gate was causing him great distress. If he could have, I'm sure he would have bolted, but he was so stuck in the mud that all he could do was stand there, a prisoner of his own fear.

I didn't stay. Even the pressure of my body anywhere in his space was too much for him. This horse was so far gone that even making eye contact was out of the question.

After reporting what I found, it took the BLM only a few days to retrieve Riley from his torturous conditions, and he was safely at my place for rehab. Unfortunately, when the BLM had gone to get Riley, he was so damaged that they had no choice but to dart him (which is a very traumatic and dangerous thing to do). It took six men to drag Riley into the horse trailer where he eventually woke up in transit.

I felt so much better knowing that Riley was now in a spacious area. He had plenty of room to run, a three-sided enclosure, if he wanted it, and a beautiful view of the world around him.

But it would take much more than that to bring this horse around. One look at him and you could see that the life had gone out of his eyes. He was despondent, depressed, and had all but given up. I left Riley to himself for a few days to settle in. He needed time to breathe and to enjoy the company of others like him over the fence.

But Riley wasn't coming around. For a full week, I watched as he stood in the corner of his pasture, head down and eyes half-closed. Riley had gone inside. More accurately, he had gone away; retreating to a place void of energy and void of light. If he could have willed it, I think Riley would have died.

Finally, I made the decision to begin our work together. I knew it would be a long and arduous road for him, but that was okay. I had as much time as he needed. Slowly, I approached the outside of the fence and stood there with my back to him and my gaze solidly planted on the ground. I said nothing. I did nothing, and after ten minutes, I left. That was our first day and several days after. The only thing that changed was the length of time I stayed.

On about the third day, I ventured inside. Riley had ample room to get away from me, and I had no intention of taking up his space. I moved into the pasture as fluidly as I could, still looking at the ground, and sat on the edge of a water trough. It was as far away as I could get. I still said and did nothing. During my time inside his pasture, I never made eye contact. I never stood up straight and tall, and I never shifted my eyes from the ground. Mustangs have a keen sense of self-preservation and are highly intuitive. I knew that, although Riley hadn't moved, he was aware of everything I was doing (or not doing).

The next day, Riley was still in his corner as I entered the pasture. Again, I slowly moved to the water trough and took a seat. But this time, as I was staring at the ground, I began to sing softly. And I kept singing until it was time for me to go. As I exited the pasture, I quickly glanced in his direction. He was looking at me! Finally, his head was up, and he was showing a flicker of interest.

The following day, as I approached the pasture, I saw that Riley was out of his corner. He was pacing slowly back and forth and looked up as I opened the gate. I took what had become my usual position on the water trough and began to sing. As I was getting ready to leave, I heard tentative footsteps advancing on the gravel in front of me. Riley was about ten feet away from me. He didn't stay long, but I was ecstatic. There was hope!

I was eager to get back to Riley the next day. By now, he had become accustomed to me sitting on the water trough and singing. As I sat and sang (still looking at the ground), I heard the familiar footsteps of yesterday. How far would he come? The footsteps started then stopped...started again and then stopped. I didn't dare look up, but I could sense that his curious nature was battling with his instinctive fear.

In the end, his curiosity won out. I could hear his soft snorts as his muzzle came into my field of vision. I dared not look up. I sat stock still, breathing in time with him. In a flash, his muzzle came in to touch my knee and he was off again. This was fantastic! I knew we were going to make it, and I didn't care how much longer it took.

Each day, I began slowly moving around the pasture. I basically ignored him, but I got him used to my presence in motion. I brought out barrels and placed scrumptious treats on them each day before I left. And each morning when I returned, the treats were gone.

Soon, Riley was perking up every time I brought out the barrels. It was time to help him move forward. One day, I brought out the barrels as usual and placed ample treats on each one. But instead of leaving, I stood about ten feet away. In order to get his treats, Riley was going to have to choose to tolerate my presence at that distance. It took days for him to make that choice, but he eventually did. He was beginning to learn that humans can bring good things.

Each day, I positioned myself a little closer to the barrels, and each day, he chose to accept my presence. We continued to work until I could stand at the barrel while he ate. Shortly after that, he accepted my hand next to the treats while he ate. And on day I-don't-even-know-what, he allowed me to touch his nose while he ate. Hallelujah!

I won't say that it was smooth sailing from then on, but we began to pick up the pace. At approximately the one-month mark, Riley allowed me to slip the halter over his nose while he ate, and the day after that, the halter was on...and off...and on again.

The true turning point, and the point at which I knew we were creating a solid bond, was the day he asked me to scratch under his matted mane. I had been standing in the arena, just watching him as he watched me. Suddenly, he began to move toward me and before I knew it, he was standing beside me. But he wasn't just standing, he was positioning himself so that I would know where to scratch. At first, I was nonplussed. Was this my imagination or did I just see him ask for a scratch? Did I dare reach out to touch him in a place he'd never been touched before?

I gingerly lifted my hand to his mane and was astonished that he leaned into me, as if to say "Yep, keep going." I began softly scratching the mat that was pulling the most, and almost immediately, Riley's lips began to quiver as he stuck his neck out as far as it would go. If you know horses, you know that this is a sign of pure pleasure. It's what they do when you hit a sweet spot. It's what they do when one horse scratches another. As I continued to scratch, he continued to show me the places that needed it. We stood there, scratcher and scratchee, for an hour. This was equine utopia at its best.

The next day, Riley was waiting for me. As soon as I walked into the pasture, he sidled up to show me his mane. He not only allowed me to scratch but stood politely as I painstakingly used scissors to cut out each knot. It reminded me a little of the story of the mouse who removed the thorn from the lion's paw and made a friend for life. The best thing was that the light had returned to Riley's eyes. He was a part of the world again, and I couldn't have been prouder of him.

Finally, the healing journey for Riley was well under way. We could now begin the regular mustang training, and he certainly didn't disappoint. He took to the natural horsemanship methods without skipping a beat, and within days, he was playing all the games. There wasn't anything that this horse wouldn't do for me, and I can't tell you how much love welled up inside every time we played together.

Finally, it was time for Riley to return to the BLM. I chuckled as I saw the director pull up followed by a caravan of cars and trucks. I had told them that Riley would get in on his own, but I can see why they wanted to cover all their bases.

But then something happened that I hadn't counted on. The BLM horse trailer came to a halt outside Riley's pen, and I noticed him begin to shake. He shook everywhere and began to break out in a full body sweat. Riley had gotten in and out of my trailer many times, but this trailer was the one he woke up in after they darted him. And he knew it.

"Do you think I am going to need to dart him?" Dave asked. Dave was the director of the BLM and I knew him to be a gentle soul who really didn't want to put Riley through it unnecessarily. When I had called Dave to tell him that Riley was ready, I assured him that he would load without a problem. Had I misspoken? Was I asking too much of this horse too soon?

"No," I said. "He will do it. He's a brave boy." But my words were more confident than what I felt inside. This was a huge deal. I wasn't at all sure that Riley could overcome the sounds and smells of the frightening box.

"I'll get the guys ready, just in case."

"No, please wait. Just give me a minute." I wanted to spend a few minutes with Riley before asking this of him.

As I stroked his neck, I told him how brave he was. "I know you can do this, my sweet boy," I whispered. "Do it for me."

I walked with him to the opening of the trailer. He was now shaking uncontrollably. I let him rest there until the shaking subsided and then asked for one foot to step in. He did it. He was trusting me to keep him safe, and my heart was bursting with pride for this magnificent animal. I loved him so much! Within a couple of minutes all of Riley was in the trailer. I stood outside stroking his mane and telling him what a wonderful, courageous boy he was.

As I watched the trailer pull away, I felt at once happy, sad, proud, and excited. I knew that Riley had already been set up with a terrific home that was waiting for him in Boise. I knew that the BLM was going to make sure that he made the transition successfully. But I was also sad. This horse had captured my heart in a way that no other horse had. I knew that I was going to miss him terribly.

Riley was one of those success stories that makes you stand in awe of their grace, intelligence, courage, and the ability to forgive.

I think it's fitting that I end this book with a poem that I wrote for him. He showed me the true spirit of the horse, and I will never forget him.

For Riley
I could not know your pain
Or feel your fear,
But I could see it as it
Pulsed through your every move.
Every blink of your eye, and
Every breath you took.
So fearful of this world, you stood
A shell; echoing the cruelty
That had trampled your innocence.
I thought that I may never call them back,
Those eyes that held such darkness.
And I feared that I wouldn't make it through
To that small part of you that still survived.
Yet somehow, in allegiance to
your spirit, you held on
To a grain of hope and the smallest possibility
That all was not lost...
And you dared to trust again,
Dared to love again.
And I, in the wake of all your courage
Stand in awe,
Humbled by the spirit and the majesty of you.

ABOUT THE AUTHOR

L aurie Ingebritsen started her writing career in her early thir-
ties, publishing articles and short stories in children's mag-
azines and women's periodicals. After attending college, she
took a hiatus from publishing to focus on her chosen career as a
master's level therapist.

Laurie spent the next nineteen years helping women and children overcome the traumas associated with abuse. Outside therapy,
she was an avid horsewoman. Over time, she began to see that the
skills required to successfully work with horses were the same issues
her clients were struggling with.

In what would be considered a bold move at the time, she took
some of her clients into the arena. What she found was astonishing.
Clients were making progress faster and sustaining changes longer

than in traditional therapy. While interacting with the horses, they were learning to replace aggression and passivity with assertion, draw reasonable boundaries, communicate clearly, demand respect, and learn to trust. Interacting with the horses was giving her clients experiential feedback in real time and the opportunity to safely create behavioral change.

The results of adding horses to the therapeutic mix was so dramatic that in 1999, Laurie cofounded Equisense: an equine-assisted psychotherapy program. The dramatic results she witnessed over the next eleven years convinced her that she needed to share some of the miraculous ways in which horses can help people heal. Therefore, she has once again picked up her pen to share the stories of these courageous women and children, magical horses, and what can happen when the two come together.

CPSIA information can be obtained
at www.ICGtesting.com
Printed in the USA
LVHW110748241120
672559LV00005B/384

9 781649 524058